Building a Home

Polly Faber

illustrated by

Klas Fahlén

For Tessa, with love
PF

For my family, and all the builders around
the world who build our homes
KF

First US edition 2021
First published by Nosy Crow Ltd. (UK) 2020
Library of Congress Catalog Card Number pending
ISBN 978-1-5362-2008-7

LEO 26 25 24 23 22 21
10 9 8 7 6 5 4 3 2 1

Printed in Heshan, Guangdong, China
This book was typeset in Queulat.
The illustrations were created digitally.

Nosy Crow
an imprint of
Candlewick Press
99 Dover Street
Somerville,
Massachusetts 02144
www.nosycrow.com
www.candlewick.com

Building
a Home

Polly Faber

illustrated by

Klas Fahlén

nosy crow

An imprint of Candlewick Press

There's an old building on the edge of town.
Once, people worked there, but not anymore.
The windows are broken and the roof lets in water.
The building crumbles away a little more each day.

But a team is coming to make something new.

Amy is the architect in charge. She draws up plans to share with Norman, the building supervisor. He gets all the right people and machines on site:

Daisy, to operate the bulldozer;

Doug, to operate the digger;

and Jane, to operate the tower crane.

Piece by piece, Jane's crane goes up. Brick by brick, the old building comes down.

The building is taken apart. Most of the materials can be recycled or reused.

Doug and Daisy clear away the rubble. They scoop and smooth until the plot is neat and flat.

Some team members come for one job and then go . . .

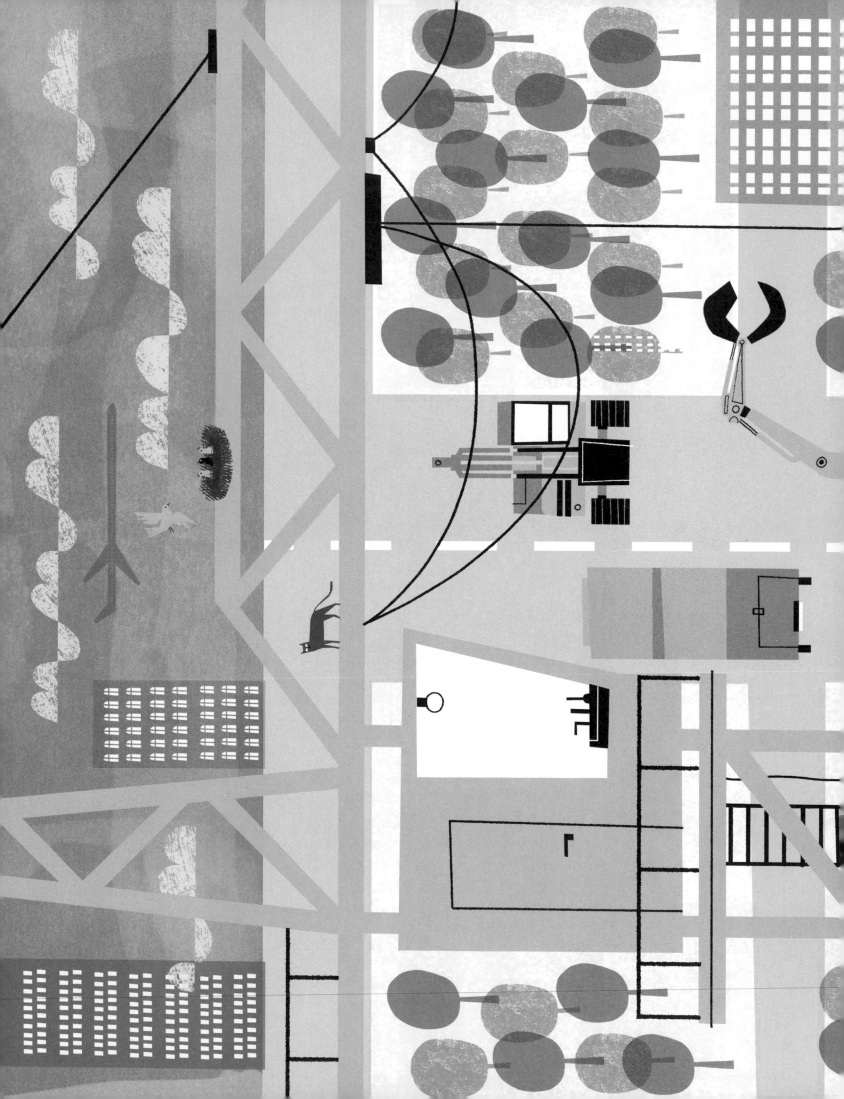

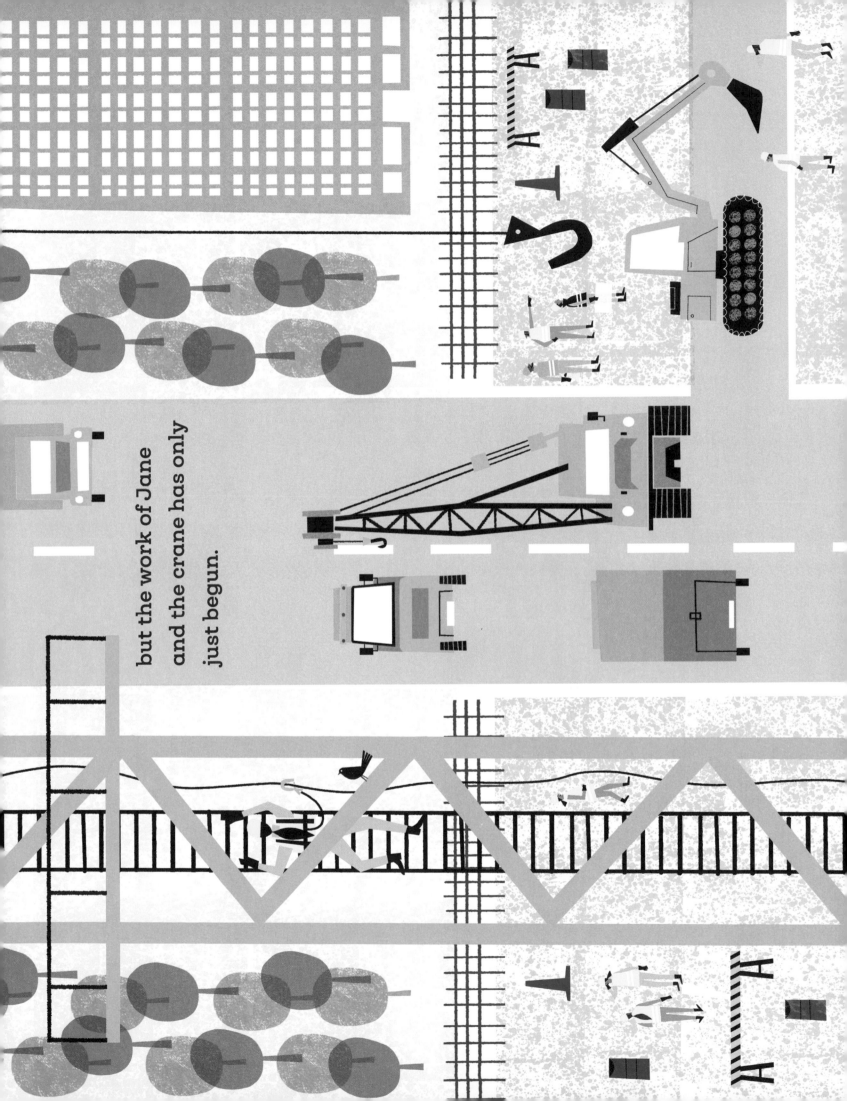

but the work of Jane
and the crane has only
just begun.

To keep the new building straight and sturdy,
it needs a strong foundation under the ground.

Doug's digger digs down deep.
Jane's crane swings in pipes.
Amy and Norman check that
everything's in place.

And when they're happy, they call for Sanjit, who brings . . .

the cement mixer.

Its churning drum keeps
turning as Sanjit pours
the cement into the foundation.

The team must wait for it to set.

17

They wait and wait . . .

24

Finally, it's ready!
The team gets busy.
Karim and Kamil attach
steel beams. The beams
are super strong and very
heavy.

Jane and her crane
move them around
on chains . . .

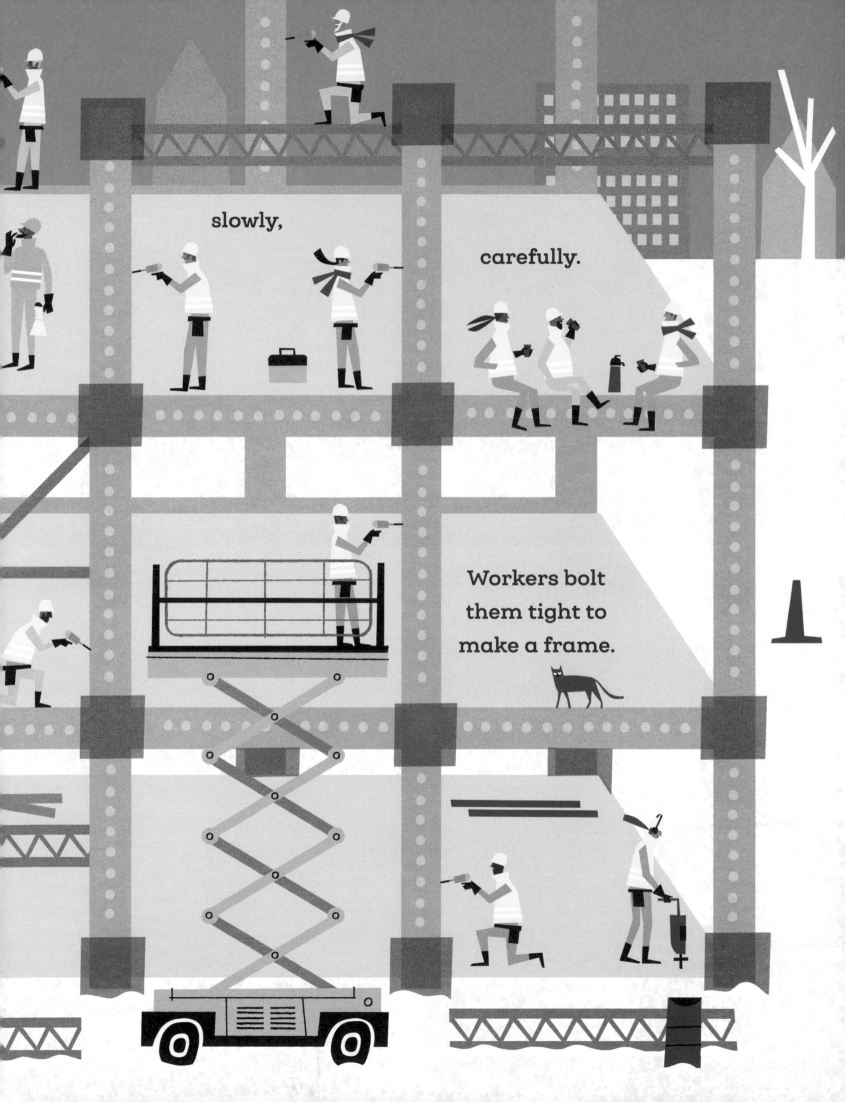

Raoul, Freya, Chuck, and
Mick use trowels to build
layer after layer of cement
blocks and bricks.
As the walls creep higher
and higher . . .

Lou and Jordan turn metal tubes and wooden boards into a structure called scaffolding to help everybody reach the top.

The team tries to keep working whatever the weather.

On cold days, they wear scarves and gloves. The building gets covered in large tarps to protect it from the elements.

When the wind blows hard,
Jane has to come down from
her crane and construction stops.

Soon, the scaffolding and tarps are gone and walls are built. Malouf lays the roof, while Jane's crane lifts in glass for windows.

From the outside, the building looks almost ready. But inside ...

Li Wei and Amma saw and hammer to turn planks of wood into stairs and doors and floors.

Summer the plumber puts in pipes, sinks, faucets, and toilets.

Maya runs wire
through every room
for sockets and
switches.

Buster applies plaster to walls
and ceilings, then smooths it out.

Now Norman can plug in
the kettle for tea and coffee!

Then Ash and Noel paint with their
brushes and rollers.

And soon . . .

the new building's almost finished.
There's still planting to be done
on the ground and on the roof.
At last, Jane's crane is taken down.

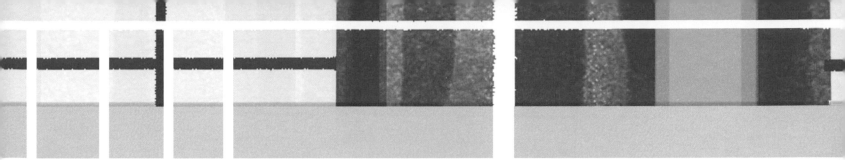

The team packs up and clears out.
Tomorrow they'll begin again,
building something different
somewhere else.

But there is one more thing **this** building needs . . .

families!
Now this old, **new** building
on the edge of town is finally . . .

a home.

Glossary

Building People

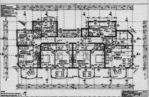

Architect: An architect dreams up new buildings and draws detailed plans for the builders.

Scaffolder: A scaffolder bolts together tubes to make platforms so that workers can reach higher floors.

Plumber: A plumber installs pipes and fixtures for water and drainage, including sinks and toilets.

Carpenter: A carpenter makes doors, stairs, and other things from wood.

Building supervisor: The supervisor keeps track of all the jobs happening each day and makes sure everyone stays safe.

Electrician: An electrician connects wires to make circuits to safely power lights and plug sockets.

Bulldozer: Bulldozers can knock down walls and push heavy loads to clear the ground.

Digger: Diggers are also called excavators. Their scoops can dig, lift, and carry dirt and other materials.

Building Machines

Cement mixer: Cement mixers carry their mixture in a drum that turns continuously so the cement doesn't harden.

Flatbed crane: Flatbed cranes are used for moving large, heavy objects, from pipes to pieces of the tower crane.

Tower crane: Tower cranes can move large, heavy building components to exactly where they're needed, whether down on the ground or way up high.

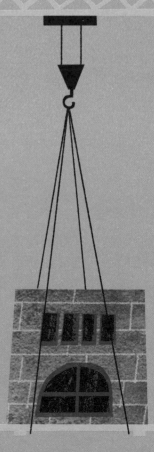

Builders' Equipment

Everyone working on a building site must wear special clothes to keep them safe and easy to spot, including:

a hard hat to protect their head,

a bright jacket to be easily seen,

and strong boots to keep their feet safe.

Megaphone: The supervisor needs a megaphone to make sure instructions can be heard.

Ear protection: Building sites are noisy. Workers' ears need to be protected when loud tools such as hammers drills are in use.

Lunch box and thermos: Crane operators bring everything they need for the day up to their cab—it's a long way down!

Builders' Tools

A builder uses a different tool for every kind of job, including:

saws for cutting,

hammers for banging in nails,

and drills for making holes.

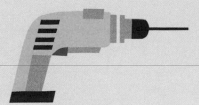